RUMI WEEDS

Poems of a Wayfarer

RUMI WEEDS

Poems of a Wayfarer

Ron Geaves

Published in the UK by
Beacon Books and Media Ltd
Innospace, The Shed
Chester Street
Manchester
M1 5GD

www.beaconbooks.net

Printed in the UK

ISBN 978-1-912356-00-3

A CIP catalogue record for this book is available from the British Library.

Cover design by Bipin Mistry
Cover Illustration by Natasha Longworth: tasha@natashalongworth.com

Contents

Foreword

Ron Geaves is a retired professor of religion, whose travels have taken him to India, Pakistan, Turkey, Iran, Afghanistan, Syria, Jordan, Palestine, Tunisia and Morocco. In these places he discovered an inspiration that has stayed with him throughout his life. He first discovered Jalaluddin Rumi as a young man preparing to embark on the journey of existence and for several years was never without a copy of the Mathnawi in the back pocket of his Levi's.

Better known for his academic writing in the study of religion, especially the Muslim presence in Britain, he lectured for over twenty years in the universities of Wolverhampton, Chichester, Chester and Liverpool Hope. He remains a visiting professor in the Centre for the Study of Islam in Britain based in the School of History, Archaeology and Religion at the University of Cardiff. In 1994 he published the biography of Abdullah Quilliam, the iconic British convert to Islam who founded the first mosque and Islamic centre in Liverpool in 1893. The biography brought him to the attention of a wider audience of Muslims in Britain, leading to documentaries on both ITV and BBC, and also Jordanian and Malaysian television channels. Among his other works are *Sectarian Influences in Islam in Britain* (1994), *Sufis in Britain* (2000), *Islam and the West Post 9/11* (2004), *Aspects of Islam* (2005), *Islam Today* (2010), *Islam in Victorian Britain: The Life and Times of Abdullah Quilliam* (2010), *Sufis of Britain* (2014) and **Victorian Muslim** (2016).

He has been writing poetry since the 1980s when he joined the Leeds Poetry Group, reading at various venues in the city and at the Bradford and Ilkley and Leeds Poetry festivals where he was the support act to Craig Raine. The next three decades saw a lull in performance and publication of poetry as academic writing took over. In 2013 he moved to Pembrokeshire, retiring to a high hilltop retreat over the Teifi Valley. He joined the Cellar Bards, a group of writers who read regularly at the Cellar Club in Cardigan. The muse of poetry flourished in the new environment and once again he is writing and performing.

Dedication

This collection of poems is dedicated to teachers. First and foremost I offer it to my friend and counsellor, Prem Rawat, who showed me the meaning of generosity and sharpened my fledgling tendency towards transcendentalist unity. His counsel has always been wonderful. Next I dedicate it to Shaikh Abdul Qadir (1900-1999) of the Alawi Shadhili tariqa who taught me intention (niyat) in his own inimitable way. I remember with affection, Sidi Abdullah Faid also of the Alawi, who in a brief moment in Paris during Ramadan, made me comprehend surrender, as I waited for him to serve me cous-cous. I also dedicate them to Shaikh Ahmad Dabbagh whose hospitality and teaching I enjoyed when permitted to attend itikaf in the Bolton mosque during Ramadan two years ago. I also commit these poems to Jane Sand who brought me back to my love of literature and filled so many gaps in my education.

Unusually perhaps, I dedicate the collection to Bryn Tirion, my new home. It means Hill of Kindness in Welsh and it sits upon a steep slope overlooking the valleys of two rivers. The sun rises across them and blesses my days. The area is surrounded by the ancient holy sites of the Druids, places mentioned in the magical tales recorded in the *Mabinogion*, and where the oldest Christian hermits of this land sought places of retreat in springs and high places. Bryn Tirion has become my fastness in my latter days. It is a place where I can write and think my own thoughts.

Last, but not least, to my wife, Catherine and son, Dominic, who sometimes sacrifice to my need for solitude.

Introduction

The following poems were composed between 1984 and 2016. They are selected on a loosely based criterion of voyaging. In Part 1 the journey is inward looking but Part 2 was inspired by various visits to Asia and Africa. Thus the poems could be defined as traveller's tales. However, there have always been those who described the journey of human life as a pilgrimage, a journey that begins at birth and proceeds through to our final breath. All life is blessed by breath, received one by one, freely given. Breath features as a theme in many of these poems. They are the footprints of a traveller longing for discovery and redemption. The longing is for the One, moments of transcendence when glimpses are given to the soul. They are therefore the footprints of a *salik*, one who journeys to seek the Divine. I hope they will strike a chord with fellow-travellers.

I have called the collection *Rumi Weeds*. I was first inspired by the writings of Rumi as a young teenager, between the ages of sixteen and seventeen, when I stumbled upon an English translation of the *Mathnawi* in Stuart and Watkins bookshop in Cecil Court, a small lane of the Charing Cross Road in London. Before I began my travels to so many places in the East I passed many hours in the bookshop working my way through the great spiritual writings of many cultures hoping to discover a flash of illumination in the inspiration of others. Rumi was the first to take me beyond the confines of my religion of birth and into the realms of possibility. Thus a door to experience was opened up to my hungry soul. He was the first finger pointing at the moon. My respect and love for him would lead to meetings with other Sufis, both living and dead. I would visit his tomb in 1996, along with that of his beloved master, Shams al Tabriz, both sites located in Konya. Sadly Rumi's *khanqah* has been turned into a museum, but old ladies still offer petitionary prayers kneeling amidst the throngs of cultural tourists. Shams' grave remains a site of piety frequented by the survivors of Turkey's once flourishing Sufi milieu. Dervishes sit in *dhikr* surrounding the site of the tomb. *Rumi Weeds*, it is then. Not because the poetry attempts to imitate the giant of mystical writing but because it is as weeds that grow around his forest of attainment. The experiences described are, for better and worse, mine, but like all such experiences they are achieved only with the graced possibility that Life provides and the guidance and support of so many teachers along the way.

The poems in Part 1 are not in chronological order nor were they intended to be written for a single volume. They were chosen because they reminded me, in a flash of understanding, that they echoed the stages (*ahwal*) of the Sufi path. There is variation in the classic stages of *tariqa* but there is also agreement that they contain love, fear, hope, longing, tranquillity, intimacy, meditation and ultimately, certainty. These poems are the result of meditation and contemplation and they deal with the spiritual feelings that make us human. I concur with the predominant Sufi view that these experiences are dispositions over which we have little control. They are gifts. However, there are stages which accord with our efforts, such as repentance, abstinence, renunciation, poverty, patience, trust in Providence and acceptance. These are disciplines known to most religious paths and, on occasion, these infuse the content of the poems too.

I deliberated long and hard as to whether I should include the poems of Part 2. The division of the collection into two parts is my solution. I also considered calling the second group of poems 'Glimpses' but somehow 'Rumi Weeds and Glimpses' did not reflect the spirit of the poems as profoundly as simply 'Rumi Weeds'. Finally I acquiesced. They are also in their own way 'Rumi Weeds'. The Sufi often travels the world to seek knowledge, following the adage 'Seek wisdom, even if as far as China'. These poems came about from my journeys to India and other parts of the Muslim world. Sometimes they occurred when sitting in the *mazars* of Muinuddin Chishti in Ajmer, Nizamuddin in Delhi, the Naqshbandi tomb of Ali in Mazaar-I Sharif, Afghanistan, or the great mosques of Damascus, Lahore and Jerusalem. On other occasions,

2

it was the natural surroundings of desert or river valley landscapes, the bulrushes in the wind reminding me of Rumi again. On other occasions it was the clash between modernity and tradition that has had such a disruptive impact on the Muslim world. The traveller sees, grows, wearies and is reborn. Both parts of this collection reflect the same process.

And so to the poems themselves. The first poem to open the collection after the three line prologue is called 'Dhikr (remembrance)'. It is the only verse that does not follow the sequence of the Stages. The poem is not about classic Sufi discipline (*dhikr*) but was inspired by a lecture given by a female anthropologist at a Conference on Sufism held in Fez. She had been engaged in field work with Moroccan women who belonged to *dhikr* groups. I have attended so many male sessions around the world but for obvious reasons, women's groups are not accessible to me. She played us some recordings of the chanting and I was struck by the emotional timbre. The women released their sufferings, pain, joys, frustrations, everything that filled their day-to-day lives in the repeated petitions and praise of Allah and His Prophet. It was emotionally raw. The poem wrote itself that night in my hotel room. Each heart does have its own song and therefore every poem has a secret. I hope that each reader finds his or her own meaning in each verse contained in this collection. They are but images and metaphors to engage the imagination.

The next two poems were written in church yards, both to be found in West Penwith, Cornwall. I lived there for three years in the 1980s and discovered a rich vein of poetry in its wild nature. Both poems, as with others that follow, deal with mortality. Meditation on the reality of transience is common to all religions. One of my first teachers was an elderly Hindu priestess in Varanasi. I was only twenty years old, not an age when one is commonly aware of death, but she sent me to meditate on the human condition at the burning *ghats*, the stone staircases that go down to the River Ganga. Two *ghats* are for cremations and it is said that the fires that burn the bodies have flamed for centuries. In later life, churchyards have played a similar role. These two poems show that the dead can be our teachers, revealing to us that where they are, we shall soon follow. They provide a prophetic warning. To my understanding, awareness of mortality is part of the stage of repentance. A turning away from an existence that only pursues the material to live in a way that is deeper; to seek the gifts of the spirit.

Conceit and *This Reality* continue with the theme of the ephemeral, the error made when we confuse the temporal and the eternal, the numinous and the phenomena, or, worst of all, lose touch with the extraordinary reality of both. *Father* is a poem that tells of my struggles to break away from anthropomorphism, an image of a cruel tyrant deity, which would no longer fit my growing understanding of the universe and my place within it. Many of the poems deal with loss, but not hopelessness or nihilism. They extend that feeling of absence or purposeless expressed in *Dark Tides* or *Time*, to the longing and hope felt in *Autumn Days, Renaissance* and *Hope*. This feeling of hope arises from the possibility of rebirth, a deliverance that arises from the possibility of divinity within. In Islamic terms, the growing awareness that Allah is closer to me than my jugular vein or the prophetic language expressed in 'he who knows himself (or herself) knows his (or her) Lord'. This inspiration is expressed in *Nightshade, Longing, Longing II* and as a response to this understanding *Creation* is a short prayer. *Self* too is a prayer for deliverance, a longing to glimpse the world of the heart. *The Thick of Things* continues the theme. Its images speak of the things that I am not, but so compulsively bind me to ignorance of the heart's reality.

The Prince of Pearls and *The Master's Touch* are pivotal. They both speak of the intervention of the Guide. At some point the longing for reality must be rewarded by the discovery of one who has walked the Way, offering guidance to the Wayfarer. After the Master's touch, *the Door* speaks of opening. The poems that follow it try to capture something of intimacy, the fruits of quiet meditative silence, the student's efforts to walk the road that has been revealed. It is not yet secure, and *Lost and Regained* speaks of when the world intrudes, using the image of a fairground ride, it compels the student back to longing for that which has been lost. Part I ends with the poem *Community of One* inspired by the Qur'an's description of Ibrahim. We are all ultimately a community of one.

Part II opens with two poems that are inspired by the stories of Joseph (Yusef) and Jonah (Younis). The images are drawn from Biblical and Quranic narratives. I was raised by a grandmother who taught me to read from the Bible and the images are part and parcel of my vocabulary. One day I would like to write a poem for each of the prophets mentioned in these sacred texts. *They would not cry on the day the Messenger died* has an interesting origin. I had travelled to Tunisia by a package holiday flight without accommodation. The coach that picked us up at the airport was delivering tourists to their hotels. We passed an old olive grove on the road and the holiday company representative recounted the North African legend of the olive tree's heart. I decided that this was the time and place to leave the coach. I requested the driver to stop. After the bus had departed to its fleshpots I sat underneath an old olive tree, its ancient trunk riven in two, and wrote the poem. About one hour later, a local bus came by bound for Kerouan, the first city of Africa to embrace Islam. I stopped it, and entered the city on the first day of Ramadan. I kept the fast far away from Tunisia's tourist scene. This first encounter with fasting is mentioned in the final lines of the poem *Renaissance*.

The Wedding and *Vesta* refer to local customs that can lead to the misuse of tradition in the context of gender. The Wedding is about young girls married off to old men and *Vesta* refers to a female body that I saw burned in the cremation grounds of Varanasi. The baby that floated past me on the river's current was female too. *Old and New India* is about the clash between modernity and tradition and hints in its final lines of the fundamentalist response to modernity. It was written after a visit to a village Sufi shrine in North East India. *The Town with Two Names* reflects my feelings on the tragedy of Pakistan. I visited the nation in 2014 after a gap of twenty-years. I was shocked by the changes, especially with regard to my freedom to travel freely without danger. I wanted to visit a mountain range where there were ancient pre-Islamic monuments. My hosts would not permit me to go there in case I was kidnapped. I was far more shocked that this ancient heritage that belonged to all humankind was being destroyed to make roads. I was a guest of one of Pakistan's religious minorities who had migrated in 1947. The poem reflects their experience.

The final poem of the collection returns to Jalaluddin Rumi. It is called *Bulrushes* and was written after seeing them bend and sway on a roadside in Turkey, not far from Konya, where I had visited his tomb. I dedicate my 'weeds' to his mastery.

My final comment is that my understanding of *Tawhid* (Oneness) is reality, an all-encompassing Unity of Being, that brings sanctity to creation, oneness to humanity and thus makes each breath so precious, a moment to savour. I hope, above all, that some of these poems reflect that awareness.

Part 1

Eternity whispers
Your name in mine
The secret of unity.

Dhikr (remembrance)

Remember

Each heart has its own song.

The glass of wine recalls

        remembrance of the Beloved.

A light in my darkened room

        shimmers from no outward source.

Raindrops batter against the window pane.

In my stillness

    there is no motion.

    In profound silence

        the merest sound.

Listen

Every poem has its own secret.

St. Just Churchyard

etched obituary
eighteen forty seven
a hyphen
nineteen hundred and ten

ringed in standing stone
i am clairvoyance

Kitty
child of Henry Mason
never departed from Eden
but William Shakerly
saw Armageddon
in the seventy ninth year of his age

there is frost on the cold cold ground

immemorial poets
like autumn leaves
there they lie
telling the truth.

Sancreed Churchyard

Scattering
        Substance
from the square
stone of Sancreed
rooks
        tumbled
into dimpled shade
yielding their weight
to trees that shook
light
to receive

shaded
in earth
bones that forsook
the fire
so faint
remember.

How harsh the crows chatter.

Conceit

Tentative her hand
draws near the pointless pagoda
her substance
suspended on a tremor of time
so slight
the Queen of Hearts quivers
between her fingers
consummate card to crown the citadel.

One loose conceit
shatters her gimcrack poise.

At the base
only the Ace of Spades
stays her finishing touch.

This Reality

A man dreams he is dead
lost to mortality
solid personality
daily familiarity.

A dead man dreaming
alive once more
searching for meaning.
All so strange
this reality.

Father

Leering from chaos
you straighten me.
Maelstrom of light and dark
pours from your eyes.
Guilt spores drift in storms
around your expanding heartbeat
poisons to quicken juices
squeezed in the vice of time.

Father
your children wait for you to appear.

I beg for deliverance
from your arms
before
the last turn of the light.

Dark Tides

Dark tides
ebb and flow
behind my eyes

I scan
their shoreline
dim
far away skies

seascape dreams
haunt
my awakened
days

tidal waves
imperil
my weeded gardens

inundate
my promises

drown
my voices.

Time

moon
swathe
beacon
    blithely
rave
    lively
safeguard me
in
time's dark see

memory
    spires
and
    lamp-posts
lean crazy
across
my brain
on a night-journey
past
companions
in
saturated alleys
downpoured
    years
drench
    to the bone.

Autumn Days

Sitting tight in my hotel room
pensive on an afternoon
peering through dust covered windows
to edifices that await demolition.

Solitary refuge
the boat of breath weighs anchor
whilei drift on waves of silence
in oceans of sound.

The night approaches
when bonfires will burn effigies.
Aestival flesh pots stripped to bone.

Coxswain cometo the rescue of my days.

Renaissance

Bright white pebbles clatter
one against the other
washed by blood tides incorrupt
in my atrophied brain.

This house is full of spectres
anger gibbers in the attic
love's ashes litter the hall
bitter pipe dreams crumble to the floor
tears cascade down the bedroom wall
I can never exorcise them all

An itinerant cloud breaks on my grief
Unbound light wafts breath like a leaf
Airborne to paradise
Settling on earth again
It turns once more to rise
With all life becoming
A breath that is solely mine

In the pendant
I am the thread
In the thread
I am the jewel

This April I will observe Ramadan
Arrive in the world a remade man.

Hope

I cling to my tombstone
Ballasted
    By the weight of lost days.
The last swallow has departed
Leaving evil throughout the land
The faces of my dead are fast fading away.

Something in the cloistered blackthorn walks
buoyed by the days that I have saved.
I fly from the grave
In the rising heat of dawn
To hear prayerful men weep Allah.

Nightshade

Dusk
colour of death
dissects reverie
Dead
a word like a stone
yet superior to depressed
drums
the dull metronome.

Given by choice being
so easy to wear
one breath is enough
to touch sparks
prick the night sky.

Snakes coil
in the garden
but the owl is all eye
In the evening.

Longing

Solar lips part
dare me
to risk a kiss.

Iscariot tastes ashes
betrays the mouth
that craves him
because he fears the flames.

The salamander's breath
disenchants
one thousand butterflies
returns
the solitary moth
who burns
to fly in fire.

Longing ll

Again it is cold outside
it never ceases to rain
no sun shines in my sky
it is cold in my heart
come whenever you want
my Beloved.
for you are not bound
like the seasons
one to follow the other.

Creation

There are two

'show me'

asks the other.

'I will'

the One responds.

Self (nafs)

On high moors of conundrum i loiter
dowse for clarity.
Scan pink-tinged plains from whence i came.
On ruined uplands begin
to walk the things of silence.
See my shape in formless night
where stars glimmer and coagulate
rush to encrust the throne.
Jade and crystal swarm on turquoise.

Snared by the binder's pious teeth.
Crushed beneath millennial humility
I ache for the shape that denies the boundaries
someday take my place
near that emblem of serenity.

The Thick of Things

I am neither flesh nor ghost
yet dance bodiless
In the thick of things

You are not my dreams
that mince scions of solid light
nor unseen leaves
written on like parchment
that blow in the wind

You are not the serpent
that rises to bite its own head
nor the ox which motionless
lows to the plough

You are not quicksilver
that measures the temperature
of all forms
but cannot feel the heat
nor the gilded cage
that keeps ox, serpent, leaves
quicksilver, my dreams
in kaleidoscopes of make-believe

I look at myself
In the mirror
see still flesh
and the ghost moving

I am neither flesh nor ghost
yet dance bodiless
In the thick of things

The Prince of Pearls

The Prince of Pearls came to me

Riding a white horse

He drank the tears of my heart

The Prince of Pearls came to me

as a bridegroom

My heart spoke

"this is how I saw him the first time"

I was left bewildered

I had never seen him so before.

The Master's Touch

Idling on a sliver

of lucid splendour

easing from the ardours

of Cupid's quarrel

that struck your heart

now you must wait

for the Master's touch

until the moon comes round again.

The Door

There is a door
finer than gossamer
more transparent than air
stands between skin
and the stars within
and on occasion
i have entered there

There is a beauty here
if your eye is beholden
to the vision
you vowed yourself

I have had to play an English air
but that is all conceit
for I have heard
heart music
life beating
sky breathing
blood–drumming of the Ghost

The taste of life
is upon my tongue
tasted in the wedding cake
whiteness of the Snow Queen's feast
her icing exhaled
In kaleidoscopic perfection
a tongue that tastes in silence
speaks
The world made flesh.

Where was I when the visions began?

Void of form

        Blackness embraced like sleep

Velvet

    deep night

where the light crackled

flickered like lightning

        momentarily threatened

to turn into angelic wings.

Who was I in this impenetrable dark?

Kept like a guest in occultation

Not permitted to depart

but protected by a serenity.

It belongs here

        far longer than I.

Like an ocean that has no shore.

Where was I when their visions began?

Not for me

    the sacred spaces

the embrace of those I have loved.

Far ahead

    Or left behind?

The Bird of Breath

In the mooncave

She speaks
with
feathered
voices

"Arise"

one wing
whispers

"Fall"
replies
the other

and slow

the seer
learns
to
fly

In the mooncave
the pale dove sings

The Cave-pool

In the cave pool
Drooped moonstone rings
Soft thrown ripples
Rock against my muted flesh
Crystal sap resounds
Splash by splash
Still waters stirred

In cool caverns
the avatar
forms the night
drop by radiant drop
the pearl star
thrills my thirst.

Breath

Rise and fall
In firefly silk
of my night
my swing
between
seen and unseen

carry me up
Pegasus wings
that
flicker white
carry me up
to drink

rise and fall

dance
the road
to my death
deliberate
as
an eagle's drop

play
your rhythmic air
tenuous
as
butterfly dust.

Caressed

Caressed

By velvet drapes

    Of vespertine bliss

unfastening

    the mist of primal breath

in exile.

Vexated by chains of incessant

words

the life ghost ascends

        to the crown

and once again

down to rest.

Thus my master has shown

One breath at a time

      Is the divine.

Harmonic Messages

Like the phoenix
flamboyant
fireflies flicker
slow to cold ash
while i await
the lift of breath.
Caged in flesh
descend to the basement heart
ascend to the draconian crown.

The journey beyond the eyes
seems a thousand miles.

Pulled by parched moons
the tide turns
breath paused
before the falling
then soars.
Inebriate draught
blow lightly
to the light
which shimmers
but travels nowhere.

Lost and Regained

Fatigued by limpet grip fists on the roller coaster ride

Head spun and back flung whirl of the waltzer

Sped to panicked sight of whip-thin boys

whose imp-like gazefeeds on the garish glare

Red-hot eyes in frenzied lust

        select their targets

Quick metaphors of satanic journeys.

I long to dive in your bright ocean

Drown myself in your love

Drift in currents of moving light

Becalmed on the rhythms of your soft tides

Listen to the waves that break

                  upon the shingle shore

drink your waters.

       and breathe without air

Drown myself in your love.

Community of One

Stand high in the forest
Merlin in the maw
A priest with no land
No mother
 No father
Melchizedek
without the law.

A prophet
    to whom no-one speaks
    or listens
no sacrifices
        bar
the will to the breath
        the breath in the will
Abraham
        Without his tribe.

A Community of One

Resolve the conundrum
    The world departs
    Even my only son
    the woman who bore him.
The piece will stay
        with no remains
It has no place to go
It did not come.

Path without footsteps
Race without a victor
Bridge without a road
Breath without a trace

Now
    Then
and even when

A community of One.

Part 2

Like fire
Through celluloid
Vision burns
Life
A longing for itself

Joseph

Familiar
with
earth's turgid captivity
backbiting
betrayal of brothers
you hide
in the gloom
wrapped
in rainbow glow
of your heart's
covenant with colour

Old man's lost dream
you spin
webs of images
hieroglyphs
biding your time
spider
to capture
the blind.

Jonah

Dwelling in darkness
whalebone echoes
ribcage drums
no sun
no moonbeams
lighten
dark velvet
tongue smooth
vastness

only
whale belly dreams
weave
    gardens
below
    rivers flow

the city calls

swallowed
in heart
of dark
there is no nineveh
        no nineveh
        no nineveh can intrude
the rise and
fall
rise
fall
of
leviathan lungs.

They would not cry on the day the Messenger died*

Down roads
Chaperoned by Eucalyptus trees
Screening the Ancients of Days
Assembled groves
In penitent prayer rows.
Tortured trunks
Riven and scarred
Bifurcate hearts
Attest their obdurancy.
Bitter fruits of bile brood
In clusters of black mourning.

Dumbfounded by the direction the death watch beetle
Seeks
Crawling across crevices
Arid earth petrified to brick
I am astounded by benefice
Shaded beneath leaves
Ashen faced front the furnace glare.

*A North African legend states that the heart of the Olive tree was rent in two because it was the only creature that did not weep at the passing of Muhammad.

The Wedding

The serpent sucked
                          slow
on the frog
whose quick tongue
                          darts
To trap a fly

Tribal voices
                          wail
rake my brain
     to spill their tale

Tonight
a girl child
bewildered dreams
welded
to an old man
veteran years
the century
span
bedded
     to habit

ten beats a bar
the peasants play
their flutes and drums

behind the dance
the mountains stand
they have nothing to say.

Vesta

Downriver
the baby drifts
as
only hollow reeds can
ashore
the fire
has burnt flesh
one thousand years
fuelled
by men
who
finger the flames
caress ashes
linger
near bones
smoke-blind
peer anxious
at the body
that escaped them.

Her fifty years of
breakfast fire
forced fed
to faggots
abandoned bones as canons.

Old and New India 2008

Lotus and Rumi reeds grow by the railway tracks
along with the plastic cups.

In abandonment with boys
the young girls play around the rural pond
until their weddings stop them running free.

Do they see the trains that rattle by
when jet planes in the sky
offer start-ups in Hyderabad or Bangalore?

In a village shrine
the daughter of a medieval saint
desires to soar.

'i want to be a stewardess'

In these words
magic carpets of yesterlore
were swept away.

The proud father who guards a tomb
has no idea

her dreams of escape

he sent her to school
and she learned.

There are others who whisper and conspire

'beware the language of the transgressor
for it teaches our daughters to fly'.

The Town with Two Names

I walk among crows

black and raucous

in Eucalyptus trees.

They stand where nothing grew

but rocks ancient

marked by human design to know

now blasted and gone

like the jagged teeth of an old man

impotent and waiting his demise.

Marks of a previous epoch, fertility and signs of their gods

long gone buried beneath tarmac.

Foundations for roads

upon which hard men trample to deny peace or consolation.

The remnant came with hope

to create from baked clay and heat

where only one tree stood

symbol of life to come and red roses.

They made paradise and hell.

Town with two names

shelter but never secure.

There are always vultures in their skies.

Bulrushes

Forests
of
feathered fronds
made
Rumi ponder
surrender.

White silk
    bends
in
daylight
    turns
purple
to
breathe sunset.

Higher
    than giants
heavy-headed
slender
    bow
to the wind
but
never broken.

Jali'uddin
    I am in
your dream
scent
the mystery
of breath.

www.ingramcontent.com/pod-product-compliance
Lightning Source LLC
Chambersburg PA
CBHW021225020426
42331CB00003B/466